CW00496588

Readers

"SPECIFIC AND SIMPLE, BUT SMART HELP FOR SOMEONE THAT WANTS TO PUT THEIR BEST FOOT FORWARD AT THEIR NEW JOB." Ming Haines, Business Analyst ~ Comcast

"Excellent book for everyone to read!!! This book gives great points on being the new person at your work. I would recommend this book for everyone!!!" ~ Stephanie Moore, Operations ~ Covenant Bank

"New Job Survival Guide is a great read! I would recommend this book to anyone that needs a little push in their career." ~ Shamika Joell, Account Manager ~ UCM Services

"New Job Survival Guide is an awesome book! Will recommend it to everyone I know!!!!" ~ Rebekah Markowitz, Project Manager ~ The BuzzPlant

NEW JOB
SURVIVAL GUIDE

How to Start Your New Job Stress Free and
Confident in Today's Complex Work Environment

NEW JOB
SURVIVAL GUIDE

How to Start Your New Job Stress Free and
Confident in Today's Complex Work Environment

SHARON VARGAS

SEC PRESS

LEARNING GUIDES

PENNSYLVANIA

Disclaimer

I dedicate this book to my son,

Garrin Jameson

*I am so proud of who he has become
and his accomplishments. He has truly been
a blessing in my life.*

Table of Contents

Introduction

By Regina Stephens ~ Friend and Worker

This is truly an amazing book. Why? Because it so packed with information for anyone starting their new or next job. I thought I didn't need this type of book because I had already started several new jobs in my short career. Sharon convinced me to check out her new book and I said I would. It took a while for me to get it, but I had just received a new job offer and thought it would be a good idea to purchase it. Once I started reading New Job Survival Guide, I couldn't put it down. It's like the Bible of starting a job.

Everyone should read this book before starting a job. I soaked in the advice and started my new job confident and stress free. I was prepared for my new job in a different way; in a way that I never prepared before. I successfully merged into my new work team and quickly developed a relationship with my new Boss. I love my new job! Thanks Sharon!

Author Note, Sharon Vargas

Thank you for purchasing this book.

I am an entrepreneur, author, human resources professional, a proud veteran and the Founder of the WorkerHelpDesk.com. I have engaged with thousands of employees at all levels. I started my career in the US Army and became a key member of the Army Recruitment Command. After twenty years of military service, I followed my passion for creativity and earned a degree from the University of the Arts, Philadelphia, PA. For several years I worked as a freelance illustrator. My clients included McMillan-McGraw-Hill, Highlights for Children, various magazines and more. Today, I combine my talents to teach workers how to have incredible success in today's complex work environment.

Why I Wrote This Book

One afternoon I was out shopping and ran into a friend I hadn't seen in a long time. We were both in a hurry and could only grab a moment for a short conversation. It went like this...

Me: "Hey, how are you?"

Friend: Stressed! I just landed a new job.

Me: Why? Sounds like a new opportunity to me.

Friend: "So sorry, I am on the run, but I will call you tonight and we can chat about it. You're HR...

Me: "Would love to. Talk to you later...bye."

As promised, my friend called. We had a long chat about all the nuances of starting a new job. Two weeks later, she called me back and told me I helped her transition into her new job stress free and with confidence. One thing she said to me during our chat stood out to me...

Friend: "Lots of people would love to get the information you gave me. You should write a book?"

I did. I wrote this book for you.

I knew nothing about publishing books when I had the above conversation. The thought of self-publishing a nonfiction book seemed daunting Anyway, I decided to dive in and learn everything I could. I was convinced sharing my experiences as a Human Resources Professional would be helpful to others. Once I started, I loved what I was doing. That's why I wrote this book for you, and every person out there starting their first or next job.

If you landed a new job...congratulations!

If you haven't yet, once you do, you'll be ready for your first Monday morning.

01. The Right Mindset

Once you accept a job offer, your life will seem like a blizzard. Suddenly you feel stressed. It's not uncommon. In most cases, it can't be avoided. When you are stressed, you are focusing on you, the life changes you will have to make, and what you need to get done before your start date. The best solution is to plan for your big day.

Do the math. There are 168 hours in every week (7 days X 24 hours). Now let's start subtracting. It takes roughly 128 hours to do the things you need to do in your everyday life - getting ready for work, eating, sleeping, fun, family, and traveling to work. Now you are down to 40 hours, which are devoted to work; on and off the job. Since we spend 25% of our week working, it makes sense to get in the right mindset when starting a new job, which will take up about 25% of your weekly hours.

Now, wouldn't it be great if every time you stepped into a new job, you found kind, considerate, focused workers that welcomed you, your experience, and your personality into their well-oiled awesome work environment? More than often, it is not the case. It can be scary. That means, without a doubt, you must to be ready just in case you find yourself in a hectic, disorganized, busy group with a barrage of unusual personalities, and office politics to navigate.

On every new job I started, I was sucked into a world which included great people, mentors, irritating annoyances, strange personalities, and the almighty grapevine. I also showed up as a "Newbie" on jobs I grew to love with co-workers that were the best. I learned from experience how long I remained a member of the team, hinged on how I merged into my new work group.

Your goal, after accepting an offer, is to quickly move yourself into the right mindset.

Here's how to do it:

Work on Your "Self-Talk"

After you have accepted the offer, how you think about your new job and what you do before you start is critical. According to Carol Dweck, Stanford Psychologist and Author of MindSet, "...your mindset is the best predictor of your success." If you control your inner voice (the way you talk to yourself), you will enter the new job confident and stress free. Focus on the good things. Before the big day, look in the mirror and say,

You: "I can do this."

You: "I am ready for this job."

You: "It's the job I wanted. I am so happy."

Making statements to yourself will help you prepare mentally and give you the confidence you need to walk in with a positive attitude and do well.

Take Time to Recharge

Take the time you have before your start date to get your personal tasks done, but don't burn yourself out. While getting things done, relax and get into the right mindset. Consider, you are the chosen one. Just imagine how many resumes the company reviewed and how many interviews they conducted. After all of that, they picked YOU.

WORKPLACE STORY: On one occasion, after interviewing, I asked the Interviewer next steps in the hiring process. She told me they had received over two hundred resumes and dwindled them down to seventeen phone screens. After phone screens, seven or eight were called in for interviews. Next, they would choose the top two candidates and hire one. If you have made it through this type of hiring process and got the offer, you were the best hire in a large pool of candidates.

Be Realistic

At your new workplace there may be challenges. The first day may not go how you want it to, your work area might not be up to your standards, and folks may not be as friendly or prepared for your entrance.

If you are relaxed and ready for anything, you can handle these mishaps. If you are not, your first days will be very painful and throw you off course. Talk to yourself about how you will handle your day regardless of what you may face.

Remember, you were hired because your skills matched the needs of the company better than any other candidate. The offer of employment lets you know that you are qualified, their first choice, and they thought you could fit into the company culture. Give yourself credit for that.

Let Your Old Job Go

Don't take your old job habits or ways of doing things to your new job. The new team is not interested. There is nothing worse than telling a coworker over and over, "When I worked over at the at Company X we had...". After initial chats, they don't care about your past accomplishments, the fun you had, or how the air conditioner didn't work. They don't want to hear what, why, or how you did it "over there". Tell yourself to shift your focus and your allegiance to your new job.

If this is your first job, don't constantly talking about your "College Days". Coworkers will know immediately you know nothing about what goes on in the workplace. This may leave you vulnerable and you might inherit the title of "Rookie" to go along you're your new "Newbie".

The same goes for veterans. Your service stories will be interesting in the beginning. Folks love to hear about where you have been, what you did, and why you joined. After everyone has heard your stories, the desire to hear them over and over loses its steam. Move into current conversations.

It's often hard to release yourself from all of the things you miss or maybe don't miss, but don't start the new job with one of your feet left over at the Apex company, the college dorm or the military base. Embrace the new job. Leave the past where it belongs...in the past. Map Out Your Commute

Know Where You are Going

Whether you are driving, biking, catching public transportation, or walking to work, you need to know how long it will take to get there. More than likely, your interview wasn't during rush hour. So, you can't determine your commute time based on how much time it took you to get to the meeting. Do a dry run to your new work site during regular working hours. Calculate the time it took, search for alternate routes, and determine how much time you really need to arrive on time. After you figure out how long your commute will be, add on at least thirty extra minutes. Being late on your first day is a "no-no".

WORKPLACE STORY: Once, I started a new job and arrived late because I thought I remembered all the turns to get there. When I arrived close to the building, they all started looking alike. I had left ten minutes early and arrived ten minutes late. I had to walk in apologizing. Although I was told several times, "Don't worry about it.", the pace for the rest of the day was off. It didn't help that this company had set up a tight first day orientation schedule. Because I arrived late, others were inconvenienced. Plus, I spent the first half of my day out of sorts and mad at myself, which I am sure showed. After that experience, I always made a dry run. You should too. You'll arrive relaxed on your first day because you will know exactly where you are going.

Reboot Your Sleep Schedule

If you have been out of work, shuffling around the house, searching for a job, and hopefully interviewing, your sleep schedule probably includes late nights and sleep-ins. Now, it's time to tell yourself to get your sleep schedule back into work mode. Start going to bed earlier and waking up earlier. You don't want to appear tired or yawn in the middle of an important introduction.

Ideally, you should immediately set your new sleep schedule to match your new work schedule. On your first day of work you need to project "I feel good, I am alert, I am well rested, I am happy to be here, and I will do a great job!!!"

Refresh Your Company Knowledge

You viewed company information during the interview process for a different reason; to talk the talk and show you knew the company details. This time take a different approach. It will only take a few minutes to scan over the website one more time and refresh your memory about your new employer, the solutions they offer their clients, the industries they service, the company mission, and their executive leadership team. Being caught up on company particulars may serve you well in a conversation.

Have Your Small Talk Ready

On your first day, you're going to be meeting many new people. Prepare for it! Have a "conversation starter" speech. Most likely, initial introductions will be made by whoever is taking you on the office tour. You may also have to make your own introductions. Have something to say... keep it short, but friendly.

You: "Hi my name is "Newbie" and I am going to be working down the hall in the Facts Department, as the Senior Facts Researcher" followed up by a classic, "How's your day going?".

It's also a good idea to catch up on the news, sports stats and/or the latest top TV shows just in case you find a way to squeeze your current events knowledge into a conversation worker are having. Make YOU a likeable person to talk too.

Get Your Wakeup System in Place

Lots of people have great intentions when they set their alarm in hopes it will wake them up on time. In reality the alarm goes off and the snooze button is hit several times. Maybe, too many times or the chime doesn't get your attention like it used to, as it fits right in to the current dream. If you've had trouble in the past with getting up on time to go to work, try something new.

While you still have time, experiment and find the best alarm system that will work for you. If one alarm didn't do it in the past when you needed to be on time, consider getting two alarm clocks. You may need to invest in a harsh sounding alarm, a buzzing pillow, or a wristband that vibrates. If this is the case, get one with all the bells and whistles. When making alarm choices, be considerate of others in your home that may be affected by loud noises.

By the way, if you are relying on an alarm to get you up, don't set it right next to the bed where you can reach over with one arm to turn it off. Place your alarm across the room so you must get up to silence it. Once you are out of bed, stay out of bed.

If your sleep pattern has no rhythm and alarms don't work, a nudge may break your sleep. Or, you can ask a friend to give you a call. Be sure to choose someone reliable. The last thing you need is to go to bed expecting a wakeup call and you don't get it.

Pull out all the stops to get a good night's rest. Go to bed earlier, turn off the electronics, or do a little meditation to relax. Whatever it takes, don't ever be late on the first day of your new job. It doesn't look good. I use two clocks and a wakeup call when necessary. It works for me. Figure out what works for you and do it.

Update Your Family and Social Circle

It's amazing how easily you can slip into a new role at home when you're not working. During periods of unemployment, I picked up extra chores, did more grocery shopping, and became the "go to" person for mini runs I usually didn't have time to do when I was working. I cooked more and when everyone arrived home, dinner was on the table. Eating out was a thing of the past. Families' do miss these extras when you go back to work.

Make everyone in your network aware you will not be available for those extra chores. It keeps harmony at home if everyone is in the loop. No one wants to find out you will not be available after the fact.

Have your childcare and care for love ones arranged before your big day. This includes pets. Find the right sitters or help in advance. Although companies are becoming more Work-Life friendly, constantly asking for time off to take care of family matters is still not widely accepted. The last thing you want is to need to leave early on your first days to care for someone who didn't get picked up on time.

Make Needed Appointments

Schedule or reschedule your dental appointments, doctor appointments, car repairs, and any other appointments you may have as soon as possible. Let the new employer know about pre-scheduled appointments you can't move in advance. Starting out taking unscheduled days off for appointments will get you a nod in the wrong direction.

02 What to Wear

Don't let your appearance hold you back. Be the person they hired; the one that came to the interview. That's who they will be expecting to show up. Having a neat, clean professional appearance will make you feel good about yourself and make a difference in how you are perceived by the employees on your new job. The key: Look good and project positivity in a comfortable outfit.

You wore your best outfit when you went to the interview/s. At that time, you had a chance to take note of the style of clothing worn by "co-workers-to-be". They may have been wearing business suits with ties, stilettos; or moving around in jeans, t-shirts and flip-flops. Follow what you saw.

Arriving dressed outside of the norm will not do you any favors. It may send the wrong signal. That top of line three-piece suit and tie may shout look at me...I have arrived. Leave your shout out outfit in your closet at home if you didn't see anyone in formal suiting. On the other hand, showing up dressed like you are going to the beach and everyone is in business casual will scream, "I don't care what you think, I'm "gonna" do my own thing no matter what anybody else is doing".

Times have changed. Companies are including the "do's and don'ts" of workplace appearance and the consequences for not following them in their Employee Handbooks. They are addressing what is allowed when it comes to clothing, jewelry, tattoos, piercings, makeup, nails, hairstyles, beards and more. It's legal.

If you really don't know what to wear, call the person that hired you and ask. They will tell you what is appropriate in your work group. Follow their advice. It's as simple as that!

Your Outfit

Select your first week of outfits in advance. If you know what you are going to wear for a week, you won't be scrambling every morning for an outfit.

Choosing the perfect clothing for your first day does not have to be a big deal. Dress to be remembered in a good way. Although you may get the urge to rush out and buy new outfits, check your closet first. Clothes you already have are comfortable. New clothes may itch and stretch in ways you won't believe. New shoes can hurt. Together, these two can be a lethal combination. You don't want to find yourself scratching, limping, or pulling on your clothes all day. It can be painful if you not comfortable and your feet hurt. Don't let your outfit wear you. Wear your outfit.

Most Newbie's, in companies that I worked for, showed up in monochromatic color palettes. Black and dark blue seemed to be favorites. I followed this pattern when I was a "Newbie". I wore clothing I found in my closet that felt great, fresh, and didn't make me stick out like a sore thumb. Leave your plaids/polka dots for another day.

WORKPLACE STORY: On one job, the team and I hired an Account Manager. The role was a high visibility with steep client interfacing. This candidate was very impressive during the interview process, dressed to impress, and spoke with confidence. Everyone was in agreement to hire them. By day three, the "Newbie" showed up with a lip ring, nose ring, and a short sleeve shirt that showed off their colorful full arm tattoo. They were not outfitted like the candidate we hired. This new hire made for an exciting day of gossiping for co-workers who couldn't believe what they were witnessing. The hiring team was embarrassed and agreed they did not want the new hire interfacing with clients. This hire never made it through the first 90 days. Their appearance was not accepted and against company policy.

Choose Shoes that Don't Hurt

If your shoes hurt, you will be in trouble with your feet. One of the biggest mistakes you can make is wearing a pair of shoes straight out the box that you have not broken in. Think about all the walking you may be doing—the office tours, offsite lunch, and maybe laps around the building meeting people. Last thing you need is limping to your next location, which may be way across the building and maybe over at the next building.

Accessorize Smart

Opt for accessories that are stylish, simple, and professional. Don't overdo it. Don't jangle bangle everywhere you go. Keep your bling at home to use when you go out to your next party with friends.

Rings, bracelets, necklaces, and earrings are the staple accessories. It doesn't end there. You can accessorize even more by swapping out your old laptop case for a new one, buying a cool pen, or by wearing a nice scarf. We don't often think of these items as accessories, but they are.

About Tattoos and Piercings

I have nothing against tattoos or piercings, but that isn't to say everybody likes them. If you have a few, you are probably thinking it should be ok to show them without the fear of being judged. Although body art and piercings are becoming more acceptable in the workplace, some organizations may not allow them to show and require you to cover them up. They may be concerned tattoos will offend their clients.

Employers have the power when it comes to body art and piercings. Major companies such as Disney, Wall-Mart, and SeaWorld have company policies included in their handbooks identifying the "do's and don'ts" of tattoo's and piercing. Companies can legally go as far as firing you if you don't follow their policies, which are usually found under "Dress Code" in the

Employee Handbook. The best thing to do is "cover up" until you know your companies' policies.

What you decide to wear on your first day will play a role in how you feel, give you confidence, and determine how you will be perceived.

YOU ARE
NEVER
FULLY
DRESSED
WITHOUT
A *smile*

03 Grooming You

Your total appearance counts. Not only do you have to be concerned about your outfit; you have to be aware of the nonverbal message you send. Proper grooming will make you feel good about yourself and stop you from being a distraction at work. Here are a few healthy habits to follow.

Have Fresh Personal Hygiene

Wash you and your clothes. There's nothing worse than sitting in a small room with someone who smells less than awesome. Need I say any more...?

Show Off a Great Hair Style

Make sure your hair is clean, trimmed, colored (if necessary) and neat. If you didn't wear an over the top funky purple hairstyle during the interview, don't show up with one.

If you're a guy with a beard or mustache, have it neatly groomed. A worker with a non-shaven face can get unwanted stares on some jobs.

Have Neat, Clean, and Trimmed Fingernails

Cracked nails or nails with dirt underneath just looks bad, and wreaks your hygiene is somewhat off. Your fingernails should be clean, groomed and neutrally colored if you wear nail polish. Treat yourself to a nice manicure if you need to.

Long nails with designs can be a distraction. Coworkers will quickly become annoyed with you if they don't like the clicking noise your nails are making on your keyboard.

Have Clean Teeth and Fresh Breath

You know the routine...brush and floss your teeth. If you have a problem such as a toothache, a cavity that needs filling, a cap needing repair, or other dental procedures make a dental appointment before your start date. Put this on the top of your to-do list. If appointments extend beyond your start date, let the Human Resources know in advance.

Don't eat foods that will leave you with bad breath. Beware of tobacco, alcohol, and coffee. Use breath mints if needed. Bad breath will affect how you feel about yourself, not to mention how others will begin to perceive you.

Some people have a medical condition causing an odor in their mouth. It can occur on occasion, or it may be a chronic condition. If you know you have a problem, seek medical attention in advance. Put it on your "to-do" list.

Take No Cigarette Smells Inside

It has to be mentioned. So, I am adding it here. Everyone knows the health dangers of smoking and its lingering smell. Having a smoke before you walk in will leave you smelling like a cigarette. Other smokers may not smell you, but non-smokers will pick up on it quick. Take some precautions. One thing you can do is spray your clothes, car, and tote the night before with an odor eater. Febreeze works well; use it generously. A few more tricks include having clean hair, eating numerous breath mints, washing your hands with a fresh smelling soap or applying scented hand lotion. This may not totally absorb the smell, but it will help.

If you are a smoker, getting the job may not have been a problem. And, maybe the interviewer was a smoker...who knows? Once in the workplace, if your desk is in close quarters with non-smokers, smelling like a cigarette may be an issue. Some workers complain to Management causing you an unwanted situation. The best solution is stop smoking. If you can't do it on your own, seek medical advice.

Companies can deny smokers employment. A friend of mine went on a job interview and didn't get the job because she was a smoker. They sent her a letter. The company's hiring process included drug and tobacco screening. She was positive for nicotine.

Wear Make-up if You Like...But, Not Too Much

There's no question makeup is awesome, but don't pack it on. If you put on your sky-blue glitter eye shadow, cake up your eyelashes, and add a thicker than thick liner line on your lids, workers will think you are coming from or going to a masquerade party. Plus, if it runs during the day you will look a mess. Less sometimes is best to enhance your look.

Part of getting prepared for your first day is packing up to go. The next section will let you know what you need to take with you. Even if you're a seasoned job hopper read the section - it won't hurt.

I nearly forgot
to take my
DOCUMENTS
and a
BOTTLE OF WATER

04: What to Take on Day 1

Along with your knowledge, and your positive attitude, there are a few important items you should take with you on your first day. Find something fresh to tote your stuff in. That old tattered briefcase or backpack that looks like it has been through a war, will stand out before you do if you let it.

Briefcase versus Backpack: According NPD Group, a global market research company, in the United States in 2014, backpack sales among working women rose 48% and for working men 23%. Sales for people over the age of 18 continues to increase every year. Although backpacks are becoming more acceptable, briefcases are still in. Carry what you feel is appropriate that fits in.

Put the next list of items in your tote.
Your Employment Docs

At some point, you will complete new hire paperwork. Be Smart! Take everything you need on day one. Human Resources (HR) will want to get you entered in their system(s) quickly. If repeated request for documents are required, it won't look good and HR may contact your Boss.

Add the following documents to your tote:

- Social Security Card
- Driver's License/ID Card
- Birth Certificate/Passport (If you have one)
- Education Documents
- Military Documents
- Professional Licenses
- A copy of your resume; just in case.

A Notebook and a Pen

Unless you have a photographic memory, note taking is required. How are you going to remember everything if you don't take notes? Although you may be a master at taking notes on your smart phone or tablet, have a notepad and pen handy. Depending on where you are working, what you will be doing, or your position, taking notes on a device may look a little strange. Pen and paper is the preferred method.

Don't Forget Your Cell Phone

If you leave your phone at home it's not the end of the world, but it's something your mind will race back to often. The worst is when you have gone too far to turn back to get it. You probably won't need to get any files or photos from your phone, but those calls you expect, and checking in with your friends and family will not happen. If you are married to your cell phone, make grabbing it a top priority.

Pack Your Meds

The stress of a first day has been known to bring on a headache. In case you need it, pack an over the counter headache medicine. If you take other medications or need to have an inhaler handy, add them to your tote. Forgetting needed prescription medications could send you running home before the day is over. It's even worse, and will be quite embarrassing, if you have to be carted away in an ambulance on your first day.

Take a Smart Lunch, Snacks, and Mints

It's possible you're Boss or someone from management will take you out to a Welcome-Aboard Lunch. It's not always the case and sometimes a scheduled lunch will be cancelled. Packing a sandwich, snacks, and beverages is smart just in case you find yourself lunching alone.

Include Bottles of Water

Pack bottles of water. After an entire round of introductions, smiles forever, and talking, your mouth can become dry. Have a bottle of water handy to hydrate. If you don't have your own water, you will have to rely on the water fountain at work, if they have one, if your near one, and if they have cups.

Take Some Cash and Change

The one thing you don't want to do in the early days on your new job is walk around the office asking Coworkers for change or borrowing money to hit the snack or drink machine. That won't look good. Have your own money. Coworkers have names for workers who constantly borrow.

A Few Miscellaneous Items

I also include my iPad, headphones, chargers, energy bars, mints, a package of oatmeal, a comb, hand sanitizer, hygiene products, and a few more items I may need during the day. For the ladies, if you're wearing heels, slip a pair of flats in your tote. Don't leave it to chance.

Got all your stuff ready to go?

make
Today
amazing

05 Your Exit from Home

Prepare as much as possible the night before. You will need to get up early, eat breakfast, refresh, dress well, grab your stuff, say goodbyes maybe, and lock up before you head out the door for the day. Read the list of things you should do to make your start more relaxed and not rushed.

Check the Weather

What if rain is forecasted? What will you do if the Boss takes you out to lunch, and halfway through your meal, it starts to drizzle outside, and you have no umbrella?? By the time you're finished eating, it's pouring buckets. The Boss has to make it back for a meeting and you have to face the downpour. When you get back to the office, you may be soaked and sloshing around the rest of the day. A smarter idea would be to check the weather forecast and pack an umbrella in your tote or wear a trench coat.

Go to Bed Early

Turn in early. Why not? If you research across the web, every workplace advisor will tell you the same...go to bed early and get a good night of rest before your first day on your new job. You will be glad you did.

Drift off into a nice sleep with good thoughts on your mind. You accepted the job and you know you will do well. This job could be the job you have been waiting for. Your dream job...the one!

Get Up Early

Get up when the alarm goes off, or when you receive your wakeup call. Don't lay there. If you do, the morning will be a rush. That's not what you want. Getting up early gives you the time you need to get your routine started.

Eat Breakfast

You may be one of those people that doesn't eat breakfast. On this day, your very first day, you should. The last thing you need is your stomach rumbling during one of your initial introductions. You will be laughed at. Breakfast will not only stop your stomach from growling at the wrong time, it will give you the energy you need to endure a long day and carry you through to lunch.

Get Dressed and Check Yourself

You should already know what you are wearing. If you have followed my advice on what to wear, you have your outfit set up and ready to put on. Take care of your grooming needs and get dressed. Once you are dressed for the day, take a look in the mirror and confirm that you are dressed professionally and look good. Take a few deep breaths and relax.

Secure Your Home

Before you go, make a home safety check. Take a quick walk-through to protect your property, pets, and anyone who may be home for the day. No matter how safe you think your neighborhood is, it's not. It only takes a second for an intruder to take advantage of someone's negligence.

- Turn off and unplug appliance you have used.
- Check your thermostat to make sure the temperature is set at a level that is comfortable for family members and pets.
- If you work nights, leave a light on so that you don't have to return to a dark house.
- Lock your windows and doors.

I left for a first day of work and had to go back to make sure I put the garage door down. I could have called home and checked, but I felt more secure returning to do it myself. Everyone inside was asleep and probably would not have checked the garage door for at least an hour, leaving an opportunity for anything to happen. It's best to be safe.

Grab Your Stuff

It's time to go...get your packed tote, your keys, and your cell phone. Don't forget to hug your love ones. Take a few deep breaths and head out the door. Your new journey awaits you!

Arrive Early, But Not Too Early

Punctuality is key. If you followed the information in Start Planning Your Commute, you have already made what is referred to as a dry run, and you know how long it will take you to get to your job. As suggested earlier, leave at least a half hour early. You never know if there will be a traffic jam, bad weather, or if the public transportation is running behind. And, if you have left something important at home, you may need to turn around and go back for it. I always give myself a cushion.

Arriving early gives you time to get yourself together before you go in. If you drove, arriving thirty minutes early is the perfect amount of time to sit in the car and organize yourself, check your hair, straighten out your clothes; and for making sure you have your notepad and pen handy.

If you used public transportation, once you arrive close to the company, you can find a nearby coffee shop. You can set your tote down and get yourself organized. You may be little disheveled after schlepping through terminals, walking, or taking a bus to get there.

Take advantage of the extra time you have. Use it to adjust your clothing, fix your hair, calm yourself down, and prepare yourself mentally. When it's time to go in, you'll be ready.

Remember This!

You never know what is going to happen after you arrive and walk through the door, but you can make it an exciting productive day!

06 The Onboarding Process

After your grand entrance, someone will identify you as the New Hire and sweep you up into a whirlwind of activity. Introductions will come fast and furious as you and your greeter make your way down to the Human Resources.

All onboarding programs are not equal. When you begin a position, you may arrive and find the onboarding process is right on target. Depending on your role and job responsibilities, you may find your work area outfitted with pens, notebooks, and a schedule for the next few days. If you are lucky, your computer will be set up and business cards will be sitting on your desk, complete with your title and contact information. Keep in mind this is not always the case.

I have had very positive onboarding experiences, but I have had some that made me cringe and wonder what I was doing there. Be observant, but most of all, be patient as things fall in place.

Great onboarding programs include:

- A warm welcome from everyone.
- Introductions to your work group and Boss
- An Orientation and Company Overview.
- Escorting to your workspace.
- A schedule for the day or the next few days.
- Relevant paperwork nicely packaged.
- A Job Description and Employee Handbook
- An Organizational Chart (Org Chart).
- Future one-one scheduled follow-ups.

You may arrive excited and ready to go only to find the company is not ready for you. Although someone in Human Resources knew you were coming, they may have failed to set up your onboarding program. You might find yourself sitting somewhere off to the side for a long time, pissed, disappointed, and questioning their operation.

From where you sit, a few things are just not going as well as you expected:

- You were not properly greeted.
- You're left sitting in the lobby too long.
- You received no agenda for the day.
- Everyone was too busy to take you to lunch.
- You have not been assigned a work area.
- Your computer is not set up.

At this point, you may feel the company is not laying the groundwork for you to be successful. Regardless, don't panic. Take a "time out" and rebalance your perspective. They will get it together...they will.

Under either of the above scenarios, at some point you will take the company tour, meet 3 Sue's, 1 Susan, 2 Dave's, a Jim, and the entire work group. All of who you are expected to remember by the end of the day. If it has not been done, arrangements will be made for your computer, email, and voicemail setup. Have a password ready; one you can remember. Included in your tour will be a few "point outs": the bathrooms, kitchen (if they have one), entrance doors besides the front door, supply room, and a few secret closets. Instructions on what and what not to do in all of these areas will be explained during your grand tour.

07 Newbie Top Tips

First days at a new job are busy, then slow, maybe confusing, and sometimes exhausting. Let things happen naturally. If everything is going smooth, no problem. If you feel frustrated or disturbed about how things are going, take a break when you can. Stepping out for some fresh air will help you power up, both mentally and physically. Here are a few of my top tips for your first days on your new job.

Be in Control of You

If you have brought out your supper bubbly hyper-energetic self to get involved; stop. Tone yourself down to normal and likeable level. If workers are cracking jokes and appear to be having some morning fun, keep your distance. Don't join in thinking you are accepted into this new tribe. You are the "Newbie" and really don't know the office dynamics. The very last thing a company wants is a know-it-all, gossip hound, or a toxic worker released into their work environment. They are expecting the polite, respectable, knowledgeable, intelligent, well-groomed person who showed up to the interview on time and interviewed well. Be that person.

Don't Slouch

I have witnessed overwhelmed, nervous and intimidated new hires, slump into poor posture. This might help you at home when you are looking for a little sympathy, but it won't help you at work. It could make you look vulnerable. Stand up straight and confident; get yourself on an even playing field by setting the tone of your day...even if it hurts. You got the job; you are exactly where you are supposed to be. Don't put yourself in jeopardy showing off poor posture when sitting or standing. Let your posture show your confidence.

Make Eye Contact

We all connect to new people through our eyes. Think about it. We're attracted to people who have bright eyes that "sparkle," "glow," or "twinkle" and repelled by eyes that appear glazed or by people who won't look at us directly. Use your gaze to promote a positive interaction.

Looking straightforwardly at someone during an introduction can definitely make you appear engaged and leaves the receiver of your gaze feeling positive about you. If you are not looking right at the person you are talking to, you are making a big mistake. They will wonder why not, and may think you are hiding something, insecure, or vulnerable. Look at who you are talking to. It helps and can stop you from becoming a part of office antics.

Give a Good Handshake

Give a great handshake. Don't give out a wimpy, crunching, overbearing, or a two-handed shake. The recipient should not have to go "ouch" because you have squeezed so hard their rings dived into their flesh. Shake two to three times.

Your handshake is much more than just a simple gesture. Studies show a handshake can improve the quality of an interaction, producing a higher degree of trust within a matter of seconds. There will be many on your first days of work. Practice your shake. No hugs please.

Keep it Positive

Don't spew out that you are overwhelmed, had enough for one day, your tired, and ready to get off the property as quick as you can to go home. It sends a negative message.

If someone asks you how your day is going, send a message that you are happy to be there, what you have been learning about the company operation is exciting, and things are going extremely well. Positive feedback will help you in the long run. Staying positive is key to projecting a positive image.

Put Your Cell Phone on Silent

A ringing cell phone and work don't mix. Put your phone on vibrate or silence. Do it before you touch the door to the office. The last thing you want is for some strange jingle to belt out of your pocket or purse in the middle of a conversation. It's not as if you are expecting a call from the President with some news you have been waiting for! It's unprofessional and will be viewed as that. You need to be 100% present at work. Especially on the first day when you have no business other than learning their business.

Go to the Orientation

It's a must do. During your Orientation, the HR Professional will hand you a packet of papers thick as thieves to complete along with insurance information, an Employee Handbook (maybe), and your schedule for the day. Plus, you may have to view the company video, get the overview of where the company is headed, as well the official scoop on company policies, security, and safety. The Human

Resources Professional will tell you all about what policies are "really" enforced, and what is expected of you in your new role. You will also receive information on how to fill out your time sheet, order supplies, book business travel, complete an expense report, and more. They may tell you about company perks if they have any.

Appear interested, no matter how boring the topics. If you may not find out that Friday is jeans day and show up in a suit and tie. Asking questions two weeks later, which were covered in the Orientation, may get you a strange look. Don't chance it; stay alert, listen up, and get out your pen and take notes.

Take Notes

It's impossible to remember everything. Get out the notepad and pen you packed. Write down the important things. It shows professionalism and that you feel the information you are receiving is essential. If you are not taking notes, it may appear you are not engaged or enthusiastic about the position. Find something to write down. Don't overdo it like you've been sent it to investigate an active crime scene.

Go to the Orientation

It's a must do. During your Orientation, the HR Professional will hand you a packet of papers thick as thieves to complete along with insurance information, an Employee Handbook (maybe), and your schedule for the day. Plus, you may have to view the company video, get the overview of where the company is headed, as well the official scoop on company policies, security, and safety. The Human Resources Professional will tell you all about what policies are "really" enforced, and what is expected of you in your new role. You will also receive information on how to fill out your time sheet, order supplies, book business travel, complete an expense report, and more. They may tell you about company perks if they have any.

Appear interested, no matter how boring the topics. If you may not find out that Friday is jeans day and show up in a suit and tie. Asking questions two weeks later, which were covered in the Orientation, may get you a strange look. Don't chance it; stay alert, listen up, and get out your pen and take notes.

Lunch "Do's" and Don'ts"

No matter how hungry you are, don't ask what time lunch is. Figure it out. If no one says anything and you are hungry, eat your packed lunch or snacks when

time permits. You did pack one...didn't you?

If you're new Boss and/or coworkers offer to take you out to lunch, go. This is a great opportunity to mingle with and get to know your new Team. Turning down lunch would seem bazaar. Save your sandwich for another time. Here are a few of my best business lunch tips.

- Never ask for a to-go bag.

- Don't order anything too expensive.
- Choose balanced food options.
- Don't fight over the bill.

After the lunch, remember to say thank you.

Know You Are Being Watched.

How you look, what you say, and how you act will be observed by coworkers. No one knows exactly how you do your work, if you get it done, if you are a procrastinator or anything about your personality. Check yourself often during the day and make sure you are projecting a positive, upbeat, and happy to be there demeanor.

Stay Alert All Day Long

It may be the middle of your first day and you may be tired but, you have to keep going, look alert, and stay focused. Need some energy...get a coffee, drink a soda or eat the energy bar you packed. I am not an advocate of drinking your calories for the day, but sometimes you when you need a "pick me up" to continue to show you are high energy. For goodness sake don't ever yawn.

Be Visible

Being visible is part of being on the team. This does not mean you have to be besties with every person you work with, but there is no need to isolate yourself either. Not communicating is not the right way to merge with your team.

Introduce Yourself

We all know that introductions, whether we introduce ourselves or others introduce us, are important. Introductions are the beginning of building new work relationships. If you have been on a company tour, you have probably met many workers. If you feel you haven't met everyone ask the HR Professional if they are available for another round of introductions.

Depending on the position you have accepted, you may be introduced formally or informally by company management. If not, you will have to introduce yourself. Don't cringe at the idea of making the first move to say hello.

You: "Hi, I don't think we've met."

For higher level and management level positions, a company-wide welcome email may be blasted announcing your arrival. On more than one occasion, my new Boss asked me to write my own welcome aboard email. It's not uncommon. If you are asked to write yours, it's a good idea to revisit the company website and look for profiles. This way you will be able to identify the writing style the company uses, mirror it, and show off your writing skills.

Email blasts are not always the norm. Workers who are not on the email system and those that have not read the email will find out you are a part of the team by chance from someone else, or perhaps a passing in the hallway. As discussed earlier, have your short "about me" blurb ready.

Sooner or later, after many initial introductions, you will find that you haven't met everyone. Don't go peeking around doors introducing yourself at whim.

WORKPLACE STORY: Once, I witnessed an employee walk up to a manager's office door on his first day and peek in. They said: "Hi, I am the Newbie.". The Manager Said: "So what?" They ducked out quickly and moved on, hoping no one saw them.

Do seize opportunities to introduce yourself, but don't pressure workers into meeting you just because you are the Newbie. Use common sense. If you work in a large company, you may not meet everyone or anyone at the top. If this is the case, ask for an "Organizational Chart" for your department and departments you will interact with. An organization chart will give you a sense of who is there, who you have met, and who you need to meet.

Remember a Few Names

If you can walk by someone you met earlier and greet them by name, you will make a big impression. They will feel good about the fact you remembered them. Now, I personally have a hard time with remembering names, but I try to remember a few key workers; especially my immediate team members. I am not so sure how much it will jumpstart your success or relationship building, but you sure will look smart.

cubicle
SWEET
cubicle

08 Office Space Defined

Now that you're in, I am sure you will be wondering where you can call home; your own space.

A few facts: In 1994, the average office worker had 90 square feet of office space. Since 2010, workspaces have been reduced to 75 square feet according to the International Facility Management Association (IFMA), a professional network for the facility management industry. Another not to well known fact is, in 1994, the private office area shrunk from 115 square feet down to 96 square feet. IFMA further states open-space seating has become increasingly popular.

Gensler, a design firm in San Francisco has renovated spaces for 70% of the Fortune 500 companies. On average, they estimate those companies have downsized the cubicle from an 8-by-10-foot area to a 5-by-5-foot workspace.

At some point, you will be shown your space. If you didn't get told you're getting and office, and you're not working for SAS, a business intelligence software company in North Carolina (the number one place to work) where almost every employee has a private office, you will most likely find yourself in a cubicle or an open office set-up.

Most workers will tell you they don't like cubes, but feel the worst are the open cluster work environments. These open groups of workers sitting at long tables are often considered a breeding ground for colds and illness because germs are free flowing. Workers also feel less in control. They can't control the temperature, the lighting, or who their neighbors will be. Many say they can't work at peak performance because clusters are loud, disruptive, and there is simply no privacy "at all". Sitting elbow to elbow with your co-workers may not be what you expected. So, be on alert, it can

happen if you don't have a workspace agreement.

Things can also change at any time. Today, you may have an office and tomorrow you may be assigned a cube. Or, your company may decide they want you sitting somewhere else and move you to an undesirable location.

WORKPLACE STORY: A few years ago, I visited our out of state corporate office. What I witnessed was alarming; endless rows of shiny white desk units with no partitions to separate them...none. Computer monitors were hanging above each work station. Senior VP's were sitting next to their Executive Assistant. Small rooms were lined up against the wall...every room was occupied, as it was the only place to get any privacy. The new set up was called "Open Work Space". To top things off, the sound of running water was piped in ALL DAY.

Sometimes

**THE BEST PART OF MY
JOB IS THAT THE
CHAIR *SWILVELS***

09 Where Will You Sit?

Trust me on this one. After paperwork, walking the building, meeting coworkers, taking notes, and smiling, you will probably be glad to be wherever you land, and hope your escort goes away. What you really need at that point is a BREAK to gather yourself, check out your surroundings, and get ready for the next steps in the onboarding process.

I have to admit as a Human Resources Professional handling confidential information; I have been fortunate most of my career to have been assigned an office with a door. A real door that I could close or open whenever I wanted. What a luxury. Other times, I, like everyone else, including the "higher ups" like the CEO and the President", found myself in a cube; which was windowless.

WORKPLACE STORY: I was promised an office. When I arrived, I was assigned to a small corner cube. I asked about it often and was shucked off by management. I made a bigger fuss about it and they proceeded to clean out a closet. Not just any closet. It was the junk closet where they housed extras; such as stacks of coffee cups, decorations, broken chairs, office supplies, and stuff. They tried every way possible to convince me it was an office. I couldn't deal with having employees look for me "in the closet". Eventually, I moved on to a new position.

If you do get your own space, be grateful. I also worked on a job and didn't get an assigned spot for three months because they had no open cubes or offices. I floated from cube to cube. Finally, someone left the company and they remembered me, the floater, and I was assigned a space.

Office space, cars, and work locations are assigned by the company; not you. You accepted the job and if you didn't negotiate yourself a workspace, accept the spot you're given. You may have landed a "work from home" position where none of this matters, but just in case you haven't, below are a few places you could land. This is not an inclusive list because there are so many workspace designs being developed today. They can be new and modern or appear old and in need of a major facelift.

Maybe You Will Get an Office

If you do get an office, it may not be the best one unless you are a top executive. Even then, don't expect to get the corner office with two windows and the picturesque view overlooking downtown wherever. Offices are great because they have doors and you can control the lighting, heating, and cooling. And, from time to time you can shut off the outside. You can be in your own world, focusing on getting your work done.

If your door is closed all the time, you may appear "anti-something" and not approachable. Workers like to know there is some sort of open door policy. They want to know they can stop by and make a request if needed. Don't completely shut workers out.

Maybe You Get a Cube in the Back

You could get the cube with no windows, facing away from everyone, that's a long walk from the front of the office, and far away from the Boss. You might have to sit sideways just to see out. If this is what you get, love it because it's where you are going to be for the next who knows how long. Look at it this way; you can goof off, surf the net, and do your own thing all day in secrecy. In time, you can also become the hideout cube or the "hub" for gatherings away from your Boss and management. Make sure you get your work done.

Maybe a Cube Right Up Front

End up here and you will be exposed all day to every worker. You can hear everything, get in every conversation, see what everyone is wearing, and be the highlight of every day. If this is what you get, love it, because every day all day you will be right up front like you are in a great somewhat exciting Hollywood movie screening.

One thing...in this spot - be careful. Politely draw a line from day one to control interferences and possible crowding in/around your area. If you gain top level notoriety and haven't drawn a line, sooner or later expect the Boss to set up a little visit with you to let you know you are talking too much whether you are getting your work done or not. Appearances do count.

Maybe in an Open Office Cluster

According to a study completed by the Cornell University, companies should tear down the cubicle walls and have an open floor plan. If you find yourself a member of one of these large open communities, you will be spending your day sitting neck and neck with three, four, five, ten, or the entire workforce. There will be no walls or doors. You will have to define where your line on the desk begins and ends. You will have to be very focused worker as this environment comes with absolutely no privacy, distractions, noise, and possibly colds.

Maybe No Cube or Office

If your job doesn't require an office, you won't get one. On some jobs you may be in a car, with someone all day long or riding alone. For other positions, you will ride to a location with a group. How you manage a mobile office will depend on the type of work you are doing. In this scenario, your work tote will become very important.

Maybe You Will Share Space

Desk rotation is not new. You get to use an open workspace while you're in, and when you're out, someone else uses it. You may need to walk around and see what's empty and make it your space for the moment. It's just that simple. For small companies, this works well.

Many companies consider flexible space sharing a great idea and it's cost saving if there is no need to provide a personal space for each employee. This system can work well if workers are in and out of the office. Other companies don't have enough office space. Instead of spending company earnings on expansion, they double up workers and make full use of the limited workspace they have.

WORKPLACE STORY: I worked at a job where they didn't have a personal place for every worker. Space sharing is exactly what we had to do. Actually, they assigned two workers per cube, but they only assigned one computer and one phone. If calls had to be made, or computer access was needed, off one worker went to find a cube somewhere else. The dominator always had first dibs on who stayed and who left.

More to do...

Although your escort may have moved on leaving you alone in your new space, there is more to accomplish. Your down time will be interrupted by "The Technology Team". Don't assume your computer, email or voicemail has been set up in advance. Just when you are ready to settle in to your new space your escort may return. There may be more people to meet, meetings to attend and more laps around the office.

It will be an exhausting day with limited personal time. It's important to stay focus and engaged. That good night's rest will pay off.

10 Taking in Your Stuff

If your job requires a space, it is customary to make it yours by bringing in a few personal items. Survey the amount of space you have and use good taste when choosing items you want to display. You don't have to be a Feng Shui Master. My motto is: Decorate light. Remember the old saying, "Less is always more".

Bottom line; don't over decorate. It's a mistake. The last thing you need is for your Boss to know you are a collector of mini something's or another. Leave that collection home.

It's the small things that make a difference. Plants will brighten a work area and are a they are a great starting point for many workers. Make your space a comfortable place where you can focus on your job.

Everything you bring to your workspace should fit in one box or less. The same size box you would receive if dismissed for any reason or you choose to become a Newbie somewhere else. Making your space an extension of your home is not the answer. Don't cross the line and find yourself a source for ridicule in the office grapevine.

WORKPLACE STORY: At one of my too many jobs, I said to myself "WHOA OMG" when I walked into my Bosses' office for the first time. I thought I was making a visit to my Bosses house, not her office. Surrounding her mahogany desk and the matching cabinetry, she had two sofas, a coffee table, extra seating, a Disneyworld picture collection hanging on the walls, exotic plants everywhere, a small fridge, snacks, candy jars, a round table complete with table mats and stuff, stuff and more stuff in there. She smiled when I floated in to her home away from home. Two weeks later, she was laid off. She left so much of her personal stuff, management had to get a moving van too move it all out and ship it to her. Needless to say, this woman went above and beyond in her office decorating. She was a little too comfy, over confident, and didn't fit in.

You have your office space, you have met many workers, you are plugged in, and you are settling in. Now, it really hits home... this is where you will be spending your days.

be Authentic

11 Workplace Etiquette

Office etiquette does matter. Follow the rules from day one and you will make a great impression on your Boss, Coworkers and Clients. The benefit of great office manners can include respect from your co-workers, raises or promotions. Mess up, and it will be pointed out by someone. Your behavior may reach management and slow down your much-wanted path to success at your new job.

Control Your Body Language
Keep your posture up, keep your hands in view, make subtle hand gestures, don't cross your arms in front of you, make eye contact, don't fidget, don't make bazaar facial expressions, don't roll your eyes, stare, smile excessively, speak clearly, don't constantly nod like a bobble head, and pick up your

feet when walking. Give coworkers your full attention. Studies show body language makes up ninety-eight percent of a conversation. Don't let your body language cause problems. Making the wrong moves can give out negative vibes and have a significant impact on how you will be perceived.

Follow Privacy Warnings

This one is big...there ARE invisible privacy lines. Never, ever enter someone's space, cube, or office without knocking, tapping, and getting permission. If the person you need to speak to is talking on the phone, or has another visitor, don't loiter in front of their space like you're scanning and taking photographic memory shots. That stapler you need...get it later. If the person you are looking for is not there, and others see you hanging around, they will call it snooping.

Lower Your Voice

There are the voices in the hallway, ringing phones, conversations, copiers copying, and more. Offices are busy, and noises are everywhere. Don't add to the chaos. Keep your voice down. If you are on the phone or talking to another coworker, there's no need to talk at the top of your lungs or laugh until your belly hurts. Some folks act like they are in their personal office with the door shut. They talk loudly, they are talked about, and they are annoying. DON'T let that be you.

Be Quiet Some of the Time

Holding impromptu loud meetings around your area will make you appear noisy, loud, disruptive and disrespectful. Take your party somewhere else; to the conference room, break room, or outside.

No Gum Chewing

If you have a gum chewing habit, you know it's annoying. Try mints or hard candy instead. Nobody wants to hear you popping or chomp, chomp, chomping your gum, or smell its cherry flavor. Don't start om nom nomming in the office.

Don't Eavesdrop

Leave yourself out of another worker's business. Working in a close environment you will possibly hear something you know you shouldn't. Keep it to yourself. Eavesdropping is a "no-no", period. If you get caught sharing hearsay or confidential information, you could find yourself in big trouble, and maybe fired. It's best to focus on your job and what you need to get done. Mind your own business.

Don't Huddle and Whisper

If you're whispering, workers might think you're talking about something really important and try their best to listen in. Or, they may think you have a secret. If you want someone to hear what you are talking about without telling them, whisper, and I am sure you will see what I mean.

Minimize Public Treats

A big jar of pretzels, a bowl of mints, or candies somewhere near the edge of your desk will get you sneak by candy eaters distracting you from getting your work done. If you must have treats, have airtight containers to store your goodies in. You never know if the place has small rodents. You definitely don't want to be accused of bringing any unwanted guest in.

Manage Your Cell Phone

Just turn "it off", turn "it down" or "put it" on vibrate". You are not at home where you can let the phone ring and ring because you don't feel like answering. The last thing you want to do is leave your cell phone on your desk ready to play "Oh Happy Days" if you get a call. It won't go over well. Coworkers will get upset. An outspoken worker may have a few choice words for you. Or, even worse, report you to the "higher ups" for disturbing the peace...oh no!

Don't Bring Odor's or Scents to Work

Odors travel fast in open environments with high or low ceilings, cloth walls, and no doors. You may not know who but, there will be workers in your midst with asthma or allergic sensitivities. You will be silently thanked if you don't layer on heavy doses of scented perfumes, colognes, body sprays, organic oils, scented lotions, and hair sprays. If you show up smelling fruity, or like a bouquet of summer flowers, and it is winter, your co-workers will be calling for you to leave. Bottom line; don't let co-workers smell a strong whiff of you before they see you in person. The same goes for potent food. Eat them somewhere else. No one wants to smell the leftover food you had for dinner reeking out into the open. If you reheat your leftover fish in the shared microwave you should be fired. And, NEVER burn the popcorn. This will cause workplace chaos.

Do Your Grooming at Home

If you want to gross out your coworkers, start grooming yourself in your space. Clipping your nails, shaping mustaches, combing your hair, painting your nails, or picking your teeth are tasks you should do in private, or even better, at home; not in your office space. It only takes one of your nails to pop off and

land on someone's keyboard to start an office war.
Don't find out the hard way grooming in the office is
a big No-No".

Don't Interfere

If someone is working on a project and you see they
are dug in on the details, it's not the time to start up
a conversation with them. Your day may not be so
busy, but theirs may be on tight deadlines. Be
considerate. Keep it moving; don't loiter around
waiting on a moment to squeeze in some chit-chat. If
the person you want to talk to is on the phone, don't
hang out in their space until they are done. Make an
"I'll come back" jester and leave. If you see someone
is deeply engaged, use common sense; leave a sticky
note, send an email, punch out a text message, or
send an Instant Message (IM). Let them get back to
you. Make the situation easy.

Keep Your Personal Business Private

Workers know they shouldn't, but many do conduct
personal business on company time if they can--

calling home, making doctor appointments, checking personal email, making dinner reservations, surfing the net, or buying stuff online. Your goal should be to take care of your personal business at home and stay focused on work at work at work. Remember, workers are listening and watching you, even when you think they are not. Move out of your workspace to a private space, or outdoors, if you need to take or make a personal call.

Sick? Stay Home

Workers don't like it if you come to work sick. They are not interested in catching whatever you have. Although you may be tempted to go in, the best advice is to call out. If you must go in, stay away from others, cover your mouth when coughing or sneezing, and sanitize and wash your hands often. Whoever is coughing and sneezing usually gets blamed for spreading something in the office. If you are sick and don't depart on your own, your Boss will probably ask you to leave. Nobody wants to get sick.

Keep a Busy Looking Work Area

Your area should not be cluttered, but it should look like you are working in it. You don't want a "higher up" to think there isn't enough to keep you busy, and color you gone. Oh no!

Keep Crowds Out of Your Space

Newbies get visitors. Coworkers want to know more about you. Small talk can turn in to a full-blown conversation about who you are, where you came from, and what do you plan on contributing. If an impromptu crowd suddenly appears, move your crowd to the to another location so others around you can do their work.

Don't Prairie Dog

Some cubes in the new modern workplace are low and, if you stand up, you can see across the floor. Every time you get up, you will see others pop up. It's not so bad if you are popping up to go somewhere, but if you're popping up constantly to see what's going on, it's a distraction. If you really want to see what is going on, get up and go see. Don't pop up looking for something that is probably none of your business. Keep this up and you may get yourself a not so nice nickname. One you don't want.

Manage Your Food

Having a small coffee maker and a few paper products is a good idea. When workers start adding microwaves, toasters, or toaster ovens in their space...they have crossed the line. If your job doesn't have a kitchen or eating area, they don't mean for you to have one either.

WORKPLACE STORY: The coworker that sat behind me lugged in a mini fridge. It didn't look so mini sitting under their cubical desk sticking out beyond the rim like a sore thumb. I heard them pushing on my cube wall just to get it under there. Next day, they stocked that fridge with sodas, water, fruit drinks, condiments, and milk for morning cereal. Their reachable supplies were not for sharing and I wouldn't have dared ask if I could house my drinks in there for fear of hearing, "NO...get your own fridge". Anyway, I spent my money buying drinks out or bringing them in from home. Although I won't ever schlepp one in, it's not a bad idea to have a fridge at work if one is not on premise and allowed. The bigger problem; mini fridges can freeze over with ice if you don't defrost them on a regular basis. On one attempt my coworker made to defrost the freezer, the water ran out on to the floor. This very smart employee had a project due that day and NOONE would help them clean it up. Coworkers snickered and said they should leave refrigeration to their fridge at home. Before you take a fridge to work, make sure you know it fits in, and that you can manage one in your space.

The advices here are not inclusive but will get you in the mindset to conduct yourself respectfully and courteously at work. First impressions are important!

12 Getting to Know You

They're Checking You Out

Before you know it, somebody will welcome you aboard. The first hellos are genuine and definitely fact-finding. Be polite, give up a little information, and don't forget to smile. People like to know you are not a threat to their position, and that you are qualified for whatever you were hired to do. Be prepared to have your work habits scrutinized.

No matter what your position in the company, workers will watch how you handle yourself and make snap judgments about you quickly. They know you know nothing about anything going on there, you don't know anybody, or what anybody does or doesn't do. You don't know who is running things, who is supposed to be running things, who gets things done, and who doesn't. You don't know who you should be befriending, and who to stay away from. Most of all, you know nothing about the office politics or the origin of office antics.

You're Checking Them Out

You need to know the people you are working with because you will be interacting with this group on a daily basis, at some level. Check out what they are wearing, where they are sitting, their job titles, and any comments made when introduced. Information you collect within the first few days will serve you well later, when determining where you fit in, and whom you fit in with. Be very observant.

The Social Landscape

In any size company you will find cliques, groupies, best buds, and office politics. Being associated with the wrong group can create problems you really don't need. It's your job to figure out which group is the right crowd to associate with. Choose carefully who you befriend.

In order to find out "who's who", learn the office hierarchy. Just because someone appears like they know what's going on, it doesn't mean they do. Every day, you will acquire more about the dynamics of your workplace. It does take time to figure out who's who at a new job.

Below are few key questions you will want to find the answers to over your first days on the job:

Who Answers to Whom?

Who is watching your every move?

Who are your neighbors?

Who goes out to lunch together?

Who eats inside?

Who works late and who doesn't?

How do workers interact with one another?

Next, I will reveal a few personalities you will find at your new job.

TOGETHER
everyone
ACHIEVES
more

13 Office Personalities

Workplaces need all types of personalities to get a job done. Don't be judgmental. Workers aren't wrong; they're different.

Every worksite is a revolving door of "people behaviors" with a fresh flow of workers moving in, up, around, and sometimes out, never to return. Over your lifetime, you will spend 50,000 to 100,000, or more, hours at work. It's a good idea to know who you are spending all your working hours with.

If you are aware of, and understand workplace behaviors, you will be better able to merge in, navigate your work relationships, become a part of the team, have productive days on your new job; and protect your own interests and well-being.

In order to survive in a multifaceted work environment, you must pull up your strong people skills, patience, and treat everyone as you would want to be treated. You can't change how people behave, what they think, and how they present their information, or themselves, in or out of the office. On one hand, a blended group of personalities promotes collaboration and, creativity, and can lead to positive dialogue. On the other side, worker actions can lead to communication barriers, conflicts, and lower productivity levels. Knowing this will help you understand the nuances of your new job, coworkers and your new Boss.

Now, let's be clear...when I write about the different personalities you may find in a work environment, I am not writing or thinking about any specific worker, or attempting to embarrass anyone. The information in this chapter is provided strictly to help you understand office culture. Common worker identifiers, spoken or unspoken, are very much a part of workplace and office politics. Every worksite beats to a different drum. It's what makes offices work.

Actually, you may recognize some of these behaviors as reflections of yourself. As you read through the different personalities, ask yourself, "Is that me? If so, you will be labeled as you move around and interact with coworkers. Think about how you want to be perceived. Make necessary changes in your own behavior before you show up on the job. View each individual not for their quirks or habits, but for their strengths and the positive contributions they make to the team and the company.

Before continuing, there's one thing I must tell you - NOTHING or, almost mostly nothing, is private at work. Understand that it is likely some will think they know everyone's business at all times.

Now, since you know about privacy, let's move on. Here is a very short list of personalities you may find at your job. Workers can have more than one or none of the following behaviors or fluidly move from one behavior to another. Use this information respectfully to navigating your new job landscape. Keep your eyes open.

The Respected

Get yourself referred to as respected, because the respectable people are welcomed, considered polite, approachable, good conversationalist, and they make others feel OK with no strings attached. The Respected stay away (as best they can) from office gossip and limit their involvement in office politics. It's for the best.

You will find respected workers in your environment. They are there. Some are respected for their work or work ethics; others for their techy skills and many for their contribution to the team. Know who these workers are and befriend them because they are approachable and will help you transition into your new responsibilities.

The Speaker of the House

One worker will claim the right to speak for everyone. They are normally self-appointed and make their position known. What they want is to present concerns, or issues, for the entire workforce. If they think the coffee area should be improved, they speak up. If they think the copier should be upgraded, they tell management. First, they make their way around the office looking for supporters of their cause. When they feel they have enough backing, they take their issue to the next level. Sometimes they win and sometimes they don't. In either case, they can be good for the office.

The Delegator

There will be someone in your midst that has risen to the top. Although they may not be the President or hold a high title, they have given themselves power to determine who should be doing their work. They don't actually do much work. They are great at delegating their workload, with authority, to a coworker and then show up to take credit for its completion. To claim this title an employee must have high confidence and the power to manipulate others. Don't be lazy...do your own work and get your own credit.

The Great Mentors

Mentors are the role models. They will help you navigate the nuances of your new job. Some companies have mentoring programs and will assign you one. If not, you will have to find a supportive worker on your own.

The Gossiper

If you want to know who's doing what, the latest office scandal, who is in trouble, who's not working out, all about office romantic entanglements, who might be getting fired, who's making how much money, and everything about what's going on, the gossiper will have the information. Gossipers think they know everything about everybody and take their information to others; true or not. When you are trusted, you will be included in the gossip grapevine and may be included in the gossip. Exercise caution. Avoid office drama and stay far away from gossipers. They hurt people and end up with a bad reputation. Recognize that whatever you have to say to a gossiper may be spun differently as it moves down the almighty grapevine.

The Complainer

For some odd reason, complainers have usually been an employee at the company for years, but they complain about everything—coworkers, their paycheck, their office location, lack of this and that, their Boss, management, their work duties, policies, and on and on. They are unhappy. Most workers don't want to hear their complaints; don't understand why they haven't moved on to another job but listen to them anyway.

It is not impossible to have a conversation with a complainer on your first day. You might be questioned by this worker...

The Complainer: "Why would you want to work HERE?"

You: "Because I know I can make a really good contribution."

The Complainer: "Hmmmm..."

Complainers always pick holes in everything. If you let them, they will put a damper on your day. When you walk away, you will be shaking your head.

The Chatter Box

It doesn't matter if anyone is listening; talkers just keep right on talking. You may even notice one when you arrive at your space, wherever that is. They will be talking as you approach and still talking to anyone that will listen when you move on. They have loud phone conversations, or they might pop up and yell across the office to ask someone a question.

In a few days, you will see that no one likes to stop by and talk to them or ask them a question, because they know once the conversation starts, no telling when it will end. If you are invited to a meeting, they will be the one that goes on and on about a topic until somebody thankfully cuts them off. They talk - but never really get to the point.

The Office Bully

Some people seem to have nothing better to do than to publicly make the most unwanted condescending, intimidating comments so everyone can hear. It makes them feel good about themselves in some kind of twisted way. They are rude to workers and tell them how they should be doing their job. To prove their superiority, it's not uncommon for them to say something to you in order to see your reaction. Out of the blue, they may stop by your space and advise you in a very matter of fact tone, "I know you are NEW BUT, I want it done this way. This is how we do things here." If this happens to you, stay professional. If it happens again and you are offended, you may have to push back. Choose you're your words wisely as they thrive on chaos.

WORKPLACE STORY: Unfortunately, on one job, I worked with an employee who was a master at bullying. One day we had a loud unfounded public confrontation about how I was handling a situation. I confronted them calmly. They had no choice but to back down. They appeared unprofessional.

The Know It All

You've got to know your stuff to deal with this personality. They're right. They're ALWAYS right. And, is there anything they are not right about? No. They know their job, your job, everybody else's job, and how to complete it better, faster, and more efficient. They claim to be the smartest person in the building. They can be more of a headache than a help at times. The "know it all" is and always has been one of the toughest people to deal with in an office environment. This is another person you may not find on your first days at work. Sooner or later, a confrontation with the "know it all" may be unavoidable. They will rise from the ranks and test your knowledge and let you know if you are wrong.

They will do it right in front of every worker in the area. Be prepared.

The Noise Maker

They do just that; make noise; too much noise. You can listen into their conversations, hear their humming, and sometimes even hear them cracking their knuckles. They listen to music (not of your taste) without headphones and are just loud in most of their behaviors. They are stubborn, and feel they have a license to make any noise they feel like making. They feel their behaviors are ok, and you better not say anything. Depending on the level of acceptance from other workers, you may just have to deal with it.

The Workaholic

When you arrive to work, they are there. When you leave, they are there. They eat, sleep and breathe work, work, work. They don't engage much with coworkers because they are always working on an intense, time sensitive, critical project that needs their undivided attention. Be careful how you approach a worker that is intently working all the time. You may disturb them, and they may not like it. Have something to say or ask? Maybe an email requesting an appointment is best.

The Walker

You will hear this coworker going...tap, tap, tap around the office in heels that do not have tips. Or, there may be a worker that never picks up their feet going slush, slush, slush to some destination. All you can say to yourself is, "there they go again" because you know who it is. They don't bother anyone, making their rounds around the office, but they can be annoying. Say nothing.

The Lunchers

This group never skips lunch. It includes workers who order out and lunch together. There's always someone that has a desk full of menus to local eateries that deliver. Those that order out make a big deal over what they are going to have for lunch an hour or two in advance. You will see them hanging around the order takers desk; the one that doesn't mind organizing and keeping track of the money. If ordering out is what you like to do, it's pretty easy to get an order in with this group. If a lunch area is available, lunchers eat as a group chatting and laughing about this and that. If there's no kitchen, they may eat at their desk or clique up at a worker's desk. They will break out their foodies, spill food, crunch chips, and make a lot of noise yacking. They have out their invisible "Do Not Disturb" and "Don't Say a Word to Us" sign out. Adhere to it or else. They can get mean.

Lunchers put their leftovers in the refrigerator if one is available. Someone in the group may be a stickler about the kitchen rules and qualifies as the "Kitchen Police". Don't let the KP point out that YOU left an experiment that went awry in the fridge or didn't clean up a spill. If you join this bunch, follow the rules or you could be officially kicked out.

The Missing

It may take weeks before you realize this person is never around when you need them. Not for lunch, not for a question, not for chitchat or when you want to give them something reference the task you're working on. Where are they? Who knows? Stop looking. Send an email or Instant Message and hope for a response in the near future.

The Connected One

As soon as you meet this person and tell them the name of the last company you worked at, which had five thousand employees, they will know someone who worked there. They are liable to ask you, "Do you know Jack Thompson or Ann Jones? Or, if you tell them you live in a certain part of town they have been there, shopped there, and have bought a pair of shoes they love there. They claim to know everyone and have been everywhere. There's nothing new on the table for them. Best you can hope is that they really don't know anyone you know.

The Manipulator

Manipulators have their own agendas; they know what they want and how to pull workers' strings. After they do their dirty work, they step back. They are amazingly good at making someone else appear to be the problem or incompetent. They stir the pot in their direction. It will take you time, but once you have identified a coworker is a manipulator, interact with them only when necessary.

The Ultimate Helper

If you can't figure out the copier, forget where the supply closet is, or need to figure out how to navigate to the lunchroom, this worker will be there for you. They know where everything is, including last years' holiday decorations. They may also be able to tell you where someone you are looking for is. Keep in mind they are watching you too.

The Not on Timer

In will fly the rushing one because they are trying to get to their seat before being spotted...too late. They deliver outrageous excuses as they shuffle in. "Oh, I lost my keys this morning", "My dog got sick right as I was leaving", blah, blah, blah, or some other excuse they can come up with quick. Don't let this be you. Coworkers don't like it when someone comes in late all the time. They don't want to hear "Tardiness Fib Stories". Coworkers may act as though tardiness is unnoticed but, it will be alive and well in the underground grapevine... "If I can get in on time, they should be able to." It's been said more than once on a job. Employers do terminate employees for constantly being late.

The Office Superstar

There may be one in your midst with an inflated personality. They need to be told they wear the coolest outfits, have the best hair looks, and claim to have "swag". They love and feed off of constant attention. If they are out for a few days, they receive an, oh so, warm welcome, on their return. They have presence and seem to be superior and admired.

What the superstar is after is recognition and power. They always claim they get the job done, wow their Boss, are the expert on everything, and say the right things at the right time all the time. High praise, regardless of their actual accomplishments, turn them on. This type of employee is known to have little empathy for other workers feelings or opinions.

Be careful before deciding to become the office superstar. If you walk around like you own the place and you are "all that", a few coworkers may want you to take your swagger somewhere else. "Wanna Be" superstars can be toxic.

The Slacker

This worker appears to be soooo busy and putting out soooo much effort, but all they are doing, is just getting by, doing as little as they can. The Boss and others know who is slacking, and it is their job to handle things...not yours. If you are not careful, their work can end up on your plate; where you don't want it. Keep your eye on your own performance.

The "It's Not My Jobber"

Whenever this worker is asked to do something they don't. Matter of fact, they make it a point not to, and let other workers know, "That's not my job". They don't go the extra mile on projects, or stay late to complete a task, even if others need help, because they feel, "it's not my job".

If you go a little deeper, these folks don't do other things. They don't clean up after themselves, they don't fill the copier, don't make coffee, and won't even clean the coffee pot. They are known to take the last drop of water from the water cooler and won't put up another bottle. They won't empty their trash; even if it's overflowing...it goes on and on. I am sure you get the picture by now.

I COULDN'T RESIST SHARING THIS STORY...

This is a story about four people named Everybody, Somebody, Anybody, and Nobody. There was an important job to be done and Everybody was sure that Somebody would do it. Anybody could have done it, but Nobody did it. Somebody got angry about that, because it was Everybody's job. Everybody thought Anybody could do it, but Nobody realized that Everybody wouldn't do it. It ended up that everybody blamed Somebody when Nobody did what Anybody could have. ~Author Unknown

The Sleeper

Sleepers lie back in the chair or put their heads down and actually fall asleep at work. The worst one's snore. They are not as rare as you think.

WORKPLACE STORY: On my first day of work, I heard snoring. I walked out of my cube and saw coworkers hovering over a worker taking pics and vids on their cell phones of the sleeping employee. Later that day, when I had a short break, the same coworker was in the kitchen area catching a few zzzzz's. All I could say to myself was, "Oh my". I was too new to nudge them or wake them up. I quietly walked out and left them sleeping. I really didn't know what to make of it but, I thought it was very unprofessional. Don't fall asleep on the job. Get your rest at home.

The Quiet One

Quiet people do not lack social skills or confidence. They are just quiet. Actually, they know what is going on in the office because they are listening. Quiet workers have a calm temperament and are very approachable. When they want to check out, they put on their headphones, hide out in their space, or make themselves unavailable to others. Rarely do they take anything they hear or see to the next level. They are easy to spot. You definitely won't find them hanging around the water cooler. Don't make assumptions just because someone is quiet. They speak up when they need to. And believe me...they are listening.

The Brown Noser

Kissing up to get promotions, raises, and accolades is their game. They have to be on top; even if it is on the top of the bottom. They tell the Boss every little thing they hear around the office, work late, offer up their weekends, and just suck up any way they can. They will make anyone in their path look bad, while pretending to be their friend. In many cases the Boss will act like they don't know a thing and can't see what this person is doing. Don't get involved in their schemes. Best thing to do is to focus on your job and leave them to stay on their journey. If you don't, it could mean trouble for you.

The Loud Food Eater

Chew, chew, chew, snap, crackle, crinkle, and pop. Believe me...constantly eating and opening snacks can be heard. It's not so bad if it's occasional, but the "all day snacker" can get on coworker's nerves. Next thing you know, they have inherited the office nickname "Chewy" or even worse, someone will embarrass them by calling out their loud snacking habits. Snack quietly in intervals.

The Non - Team Player

You may or may not spot an employee wearing this label. They're the one that won't help or make sacrifices for the team. They do not appear to be committed or enthusiastic about their job. They stay grounded on their own little island. Successful workers merge into their team and function as an active participant. Be a team player!

A Few Thoughts...

I am sure you have a few quirks of your own to consider stopping. Please do. You will be appreciated and gain a good reputation if you don't take your obnoxious behaviors to the office and are always considerate of others. If you are open and not judgmental, you will find yourself in good shape.

Always remember it takes a multitude of personalities to get the job done. Make sure you are a contributor to the success of your team and company.

14 Merge In

Here's the thing, you are the Newbie and there is no way around it. Some workers will welcome you more than others and you should know that up front. You are literally walking into the unknown, hoping people like you and that you will work well on your assigned team, grasp the lay of the land quickly, and excel.

Understand that YOU, showing up constitutes change to what may be perceived as an already cohesive team with roles assigned, hierarchies, established social groups and responsibilities. Workers may not want their team disturbed. Just like you have to merge in, your new work team will also be making adjustments because you have arrived.

Of course, the length of time it takes to merge into a work group varies. While you may fit in immediately at some jobs, it may take longer at others. So, roll up your sleeves and get busy soaking up all the information you can about coworkers and how they are moving around doing the work they do. Be assured you are not the first Newbie to show up and you will not be the last one. What you want is to become a valuable team player, get along with everyone, avoid confrontation, bond with your Boss, and avoid stressful situations. Here are my top tips.

Check Yourself First

Now that you know many of the behaviors you may find in your new work place, think about your own. Leave your quirky, obnoxious habits at home and you won't disturb or annoy others. The last thing you want is to be given one of those snarky nicknames, and to find yourself an outsider who is inside the team. It's understood that we are all individuals with different habits, but make sure yours are the ones that coworkers can tolerate.

Be Ready to Adapt

Your environment is new and finding your place is the challenge. After your first day, you may leave with doubts, compare where you were to where you are, or have other judgments; some good and maybe some not so good. You will notice things are not done the same, the people and personalities are different, and believe it or not, you may miss a few folks from your old crowd at the old job.

Over time, you will gather enough information to figure out how your new job works, who's there and where you fit in. You will make choices, begin to connect with coworkers, ask questions and, dig in to your new responsibilities.

Take it one day at a time. Don't rush things. Before you know it, you will be folded in. The key is realizing you will need to adapt to change and pass through stages to merge in.

Be A Class Act

Be someone to emulate; someone that has high standards and the ability to make others feel comfortable in your presence. Treat co-workers as you would like to be treated. Smirking, shouting, demeaning, gossiping, smart mouthing, and not acting professional is not acceptable.

Be Available

You can't sink into the office décor and expect to thrive. Get to know your coworkers. Being friendly, and approachable will help you get settled in. Let them know you want to be on the team.

Don't miss chances to network. Walk about and meet the people you didn't meet. Being glued to your seat, like you are on watch for some big event, only shows that you may be standoffish and not confident.

Start with the people that are working closest to you. If you haven't met them all; introduce yourself. Be pleasant so it is clear you want to be excepted.

Listen More-Talk Less

Observing and listening, without running off at the mouth, is hard to do when you feel you have so much to offer. Realize you don't know what you don't know. Going in with all the answers, is not the answer. Give yourself time to learn the job. You have to know how things are done, the processes used, and office protocol before you can chime in and grand stand about what you know or will bring to the table. Don't get ahead of yourself.

Avoid Gossip

Don't get drawn into the chitter-chatter of gossipers; smile, nod, or bite your tongue if you have to. When you talk about coworkers behind their backs, discuss their work or personal life, it can't lead to anything good. Let the gossiper think you are a good listener, but by all means, don't consider anything you hear as gospel. Move on quickly.

Choose Associations Wisely

Avoid joining cliques, sharing confidences, or adopting a permanent lunch group until you know who you are working with and what your responsibilities are. You won't be doing yourself any favors rushing into what you think are friendships and then find out later they are not as friendly as they appear. That seemingly rude person could just be shy while that sweet, helpful person could be the office toxic worker.

Learn How Things Work

No matter where you work or what you do, there are tools of your trade. It is possible you will come across equipment that you've never worked with before, software programs you didn't know existed, or processes that seem far more complex than you thought they would be. The last thing you need is to hurt yourself, someone else, or delete critical data. And, you don't want to break anything. All copy machines are not as equal as you may think.

Don't forget to take notes when you are being trained. Coworkers stopping what they are doing to give you instructions over and over may get frustrated and consider you as a slow learner.

Find a Buddy

Hopefully, your personality will click with someone on your team. "The One" is not really easy to find, but once you do, they will help you navigate the office, bring you up to date on projects, give you inside information, and help you understand the office politics. Your buddy will be there for the small things that will ease your transition into your new job. You'll know when you find one.

Ask Questions

On your first days, you will have questions. Don't be afraid to ask them. It's important to understand how things work, who's who, and how you can make a positive impact.

Here are a few questions to get you started asking what you need to know.

You: What is the top project the team is working on?

You: Is there any materials I can read in advance?

You: Are there any upcoming meetings I can attend?

You: What software programs are you using?

You: Are there any issues I should be aware of?

It's a top priority to do your job at the highest level. If you are unclear about directions you are given, ask follow-up questions. Here are a few...

You: "I'm sorry, I didn't quite get how you would like me to proceed on..."

You: "Can you please explain..."

You: "I understand the first concept, but I..."

Slow Down

It's tempting to want to get up and running quickly but slow it down and focus on getting acclimated to the team and the work. When given a task, work on it consistently and produce the results your Boss is looking for.

Respect Coworkers Expertise

As you begin to get assignments, collaborate with co-workers. Ask for their input or advice when something comes up in their realm of expertise. They'll appreciate being consulted, and you'll learn something. Most people want to be heard, valued, and validated.

Manage Your Files

You will have several key documents to keep in a safe place: Offer Letter, Benefit Documents, Employee Handbook, and by all means your Job Description. If you didn't receive these documents, ask for them.

If you haven't received a job description, don't be shy; draft your own and email it to the Boss and/or Human Resources. Ask if any changes need to be made. This is an extremely important document that you can use when preparing for your performance review or when requesting a raise. Keep emails of praise you receive from your manager, coworkers, clients, or others. In a safe place.

If things start to go awry, keep notes on the situation. I often, email myself notes on situations that occur or blind copy myself on emails if I think are important. If things improve, great, if they don't, you have a record of events. Sorry, I don't want to dampen your enthusiasm for your new role but, many workers don't have needed documentation to prove their situation. Don't let that be you.

TOP TIP

Use common sense and be mindful of others. Never be disruptive offensive, or a nuisance. Consider the positive, communicate effectively, never assume anything, be flexible, and don't jump to conclusions.

15 Should I Say That?

Keep it professional. Don't get comfy and start saying things you shouldn't at work. This is so important I had to devote a section to covering the subject. The list below seems small, but it's huge when it comes to merging in. Losing control of your language filters is NOT good and NOT the image you want to portray at the office. Here are my top comments on communications you don't want to use.

Cursing

Cussing, swearing, insulting, abusive, or crude language - whatever you want to call it – is offensive and has no place at work. The style of communication will bring your professionalism into question, have an impact on how you are perceived, and could stunt your career growth.

There are a few - only a few - companies that view cursing as positive. They claim it shows workers are passionate about their work and open towards each other. Some say profanity motivates certain workers to get their jobs done. Most companies don't share this view, and some have strict "no profanity" policies. If a worker crosses the line, a disgruntled worker can accuse the company of harassment sending them right into a legal whirlwind. Never curse at work.

Using Slang Phrases

Street style slang might offend or be misinterpreted. Keep your conversation professional or you can get labeled as too trendy or unsophisticated. Here are a few phrases that may work with your personal social crowd, but not on the job...."That sucks.", "They are so lame.", "This is so sick.", "He's such a noser", "That's so hot!", or "Yo" for hi. And please, if you are a mid-career worker, don't try to use current street slang or try to interject an old school phrase like, "That's cool or groovy." into a conversation. Use conventional English. Here are a few more phrases you don't want to use at your new job:

"You Guys" or "Ya'll"

If you want to be, and remain an outsider, call your coworkers, "You guys". This phrase may backfire into a "them against you", which will alienate you from the team. And, it doesn't sound good. A woman in the room may belt out they are not "one of the guys". It not ok to use this tidbit of slang.

The last thing I want to hear from a Newbie is "I think I am "gonna" like working with "ya'll". It makes me want to cringe and feel like we, the workers, are part of a herd they are entering. Use an alternative; Everyone, Everybody, or Team.

"In my opinion..."

You are not in a position on day one, two, three, four, or even day five, to have an opinion. You just arrived. How can you have an opinion on anything in a few days? That's what your coworkers will be thinking. Someone may blurt out, "Your opinions don't' count right now...you don't know the history of this project". Get to know the project specifics and how they work before you give your take on how something should be done.

"It is what it is."

Although the world is embracing philosophical Zen habits, uttering out this phrase will make a few heads turn. Although you may have good intentions in your quest to say a situation is beyond your control, this cliché phrase sounds like you are willing to settle or make do with less than you need.

Business Slang/Jargon

Some "businessy" phrases may make you sound out of touch if it's not verbiage usually used in your new workplace. Vague language such as "value-add", "deep dive", "streamline", "due diligence", "take it to the next level" or "360-degree-thinking" are words that may not give clarity. Be careful using empty old school workplace slang.

Eye Talking

Staring, furrowing your brow, eye rolling, or avoiding eye contact are communications that can be read by others. A hundred years ago during the Shakespearian period, these eye movements may have been used as a positive display of passion and approval. Today, they can display disapproval; especially at work.

Best advice...use traditional English.

go the
Extra mile,
it's never
Crowded.

16 The New Boss

I cannot end this book without adding a section about your "New Boss".

Every time you walk into a job as a Newbie you will get one. Your relationship with the Boss is key to your success at work. You can do all the homework you are told to do in many books: meet a few workers before you start, ask questions, surf the internet looking for the soft skills associated with your Boss, and more. Doing so will be helpful, but you really don't know how your relationship will develop until you get there.

Keep in mind, you are not familiar with them, and they are not familiar with you; it's a clean slate for both. Getting to know your new Boss and gaining their acceptance can be the beginning of new opportunities. If it doesn't happen, it can be the demise of your career at the new company. Take the time to build rapport and establish a sense of connection through communication.

All Bosses are not equal. If you work long enough, you are bound to encounter all types with changing management styles. Some Bosses change from minute to minute. They may be Mr. Smarts in the morning, James by afternoon, and down to Jimmy by close of business. Keep your eyes open.

If you're lucky enough to get a boss that is a great communicator, relationship builder, and who shows genuine interest that you have joined the team; you will be off to a great start. There really isn't much to say about this type of Boss. You will recognize them immediately. As you move through your first days, they will inspire and motivate you, as well as help you navigate your new responsibilities.

I have reported to supportive bosses, micro-managers, non-existent bosses, ones that threw me under the, and ones who embarrassed me in front of my peers. I have had bosses motivated by Disney, prestige, their titles, and their car in the parking lot. One, I had a boss that asked me to buy stuff for them; spy on employees as well as help plan their wedding during work hours.

Key Advice

Tip: Never be bullied by your Boss; stand up for yourself in a professional manner. Don't cower. If the bullying starts on day one, and you let it go, you will suffer silently until you find a new job.

First Encounter with the New Boss

You probably met your Boss, along with other key company stakeholders, during the interview process. Your initial meeting with the perspective Boss definitely included probing questions, but the real deal is they were checking you out to see if you will be a fit in. Before you were hired, they collaborated, and agreed to make you an offer.

Fit in...exactly what does that mean? Who knows? Here's my take. If the Boss is the absent manager type, they may want to probe see if you can work independently or will you need hand holding. If they are a "Bossy Boss", they may want to identify if you can be screamed at and still perform. They may be checking to see if you are too "nicety" or stuck on yourself. If you have made it by the Boss, consider you have met the "fit in" challenge.

Observe Their Style

Once on the job, pay close attention to your Boss's style. Are they leaving things up to the team, micro-managing, shouting, digging into their work, open to conversation, giving clear direction, meeting deadlines, rushing, never in, approachable, unapproachable, rude, staying late, arriving early, or have their door closed most of the time?

Knowing these behaviors will help you understand what drives them. When you know something about how they operate, you can align with their behaviors and priorities to mirror theirs.   Ease on In

If you start from day one, building a good reputation around the office and showing you're engaged in what's going on, your new Boss will see you as an important addition to the team. Over time, they will include you in key projects, which could lead to future promotions and a raise.

Always keep in mind your Boss is in their position because someone selected them for their role and they are not likely leaving because you showed up. Stay open minded, don't be fake, be you, do sweat some of the small stuff, have a good attitude, do your work, and build a positive relationship with them. It may not be easy, but it can be done. If you don't, survival on your new job could have toxic consequences to deal with.

One Last Thing

A good book is a good book.
~ Malorie Blackman, Actress

Armed with all the information in this book, you can now walk right into your new job with confidence, have an idea of who is in there, and know how to manage yourself to become the successful contributing team member you want to be. It's not an all-inclusive guide, but there is enough here to get you thinking, about yourself and how you will merge into your new job.

No matter who you are or what role you are filling; you're bound to have good and not so good days. Accept it, take deep breaths, wipe your slate clean, and start all over tomorrow. Take one day at a time.

Acknowledgements

This book is the result of contributions of many wonderful people that I have come into contact with during my life journey. All have been my inspiration.

My Family: Garrin (my Son), Gregory (my Brother), Sonny, (my Brother), Reese (my Man), Stephanie (my Awesome Daughter–in-Law), Autumn (the Best Young Lady in My Life), Aaliyah (my Sweetie Pie), I thank you all for sharing your journey with me.

My Parents and Grandparents: Mommy, Mom, Pop and Daddy, I know you are looking down on me and proud that I have published this book. They were all workers and I weave their experiences into this book.

My Best Friends: Geneva J., Denise C., Linda W. and Linda R., Gail T. and Kim E. have always been there for me and have supported me throughout my life.

My Editor: Ming Hines, who read/re-read my book and helped me find typo and grammar error.

My Journey Coworkers: Over my long career, I have made many friends and stay in touch with them on a regular basis. All shaped my career in some way.

My Applabs Coworkers: Stephanie M., Malek K., and Lynn H. who encouraged me to keep going in my quest to learn how to publish my writings.

My Work Mentors: General Ono (US Army) John Roska (Roska Direct, Inc.), Farid Naib (FNX Solutions), Gail Inderweis (Keystone Care, Inc.), Sashi Reddi (Applabs/CSC/SRI Capital), Jatin Metha, (Metasense, Inc.), Dr. Ted Emmitt and Dr. Fran Barg (University of Pennsylvania). I admire their success.

My Daniel D. Dowling Ambler Legion #769 Family: A team of friendships that I cherish.

Review Request

If you have found something useful in this book, please stop over at amazon.com/author/svargas, click on the New Job Survival Guide and write a review. Your review will help me reach workers starting their new or next job. Thank you!

More Books by Sharon Vargas

Get them on Amazon

The Interview Survival Guide

The Layoff Survival Guide

STAY CONNECTED

Contact Sharon Vargas: info@sharonvargas.com

Twitter: https://twitter.com/workhelpdesk

Visit: WorkerHelpDesk.com

22013709R00088

Printed in Great Britain
by Amazon